MARTIN HEIDEGGER

WHAT IS PHILOSOPHY?

D1593332

Translated with an Introduction

by

WILLIAM KLUBACK and JEAN T. WILDE

COLLEGE & UNIVERSITY PRESS · *Publishers*

NEW HAVEN, CONN.

Vortrag, gehalten in Cerisy-la-Salle / Normandie

im August 1955 zur Einleitung eines Gespräches

ACKNOWLEDGMENTS

It is impossible to express adequately our gratitude to Professor William Kimmel whose scholarship and understanding made this book possible. We are grateful to Professor Adelaide Simpson who generously and carefully checked the Greek words and phrases in the text.

MANUFACTURED IN THE UNITED STATES OF AMERICA BY
UNITED PRINTING SERVICES, INC.
NEW HAVEN, CONN.

To Dino Bigongiari

SELECTED BIBLIOGRAPHY OF
HEIDEGGER'S WORKS

Sein und Zeit. Halle, 1927.

Kant und das Problem der Metaphysik. Frankfurt, 1951.

Vom Wesen des Grundes. Frankfurt, 1948.

Was ist Metaphysik? Frankfurt, 1949.

Platons Lehre von der Wahrheit, mit einem Brief über den Humanismus. Bern, 1954.

Holzwege. Frankfurt, 1950.

Vom Wesen der Wahrheit. Frankfurt, 1949.

Was ist das—die Philosophie? Pfullingen, 1956.

Einführung in die Metaphysik. Tübingen, 1953.

Zur Seinsfrage. Frankfurt, 1956.

Erläuterung zu Hölderlins Dichtung. Frankfurt, 1951.

Was heisst Denken? Tübingen, 1954.

Der Satz vom Grund. Pfullingen, 1957.

Hebel—Der Hausfreund. Pfullingen, 1957.

Vorträge und Aufsätze. Pfullingen, 1954.

Introduction

The direction of Martin Heidegger's thought is not a peculiar phenomenon, nor is it radically new. This does not mean that Heidegger's thought is not one of the most significant and meaningful reinterpretations of Western European thinking. It is. The Heideggerian religiosity breathes deeply the air of Böhme and of Pietism. Most striking is the resemblance of Heidegger's thought to Schelling's Berlin lectures of 1840-41 in which the powerful influence of Schleiermacher had overwhelmed the Spinosistic and Hegelian roots of Schelling. What must be clarified in any introduction to Heidegger is that this thinker is dominated and

decisively determined by the distinctive nature of German thought from Luther through Böhme, Romanticism and vitalism. Nevertheless Heidegger's position is individual and it is this individuality which must be elucidated.[1]

The translation of *Was ist das—die Philosophie?* offers clues to Heidegger's reinterpretation of philosophy and his attempt to redirect philosophic thought into more fruitful directions. He is concerned with the fact that philosophy has lost its receptivity to the Being of being.[2] In other words, philosophy no longer seeks the groundless ground of Being which allows us to ask meaningful questions about being or its appearances. Heidegger uses Being as the "inner light," that illumination through which we become conscious

---

1. A full treatment of Heidegger's position will be offered in a forthcoming volume being prepared by the present authors in collaboration with Professor William Kimmel of Hunter College. The volume will be entitled *The Search for Being*.

2. *Sein*, Being, is that permanent reality within being which endures and remains and finally disposes us to the meaning of being (*Seiendes*) or appearance. Thus the necessary distinction between Being with a capital "B" and being with a small "b."

of our meaning or of our existence and of existence itself. The light allows us to know that we are beings. It illumines the ground which makes this knowledge possible. We come to be as *Dasein,* the human reality, through which we become known to ourselves. The Heideggerian approach forces us to return, and this path of return leads to a correspondence with the source and primordial structure of all being, the Being of being. Man must seek himself in the ground of life, the *Ungrund,* the Being of beings. In man's seeking and his grasping of the nature of Being the structure of his meaning and the nature of human reality become clearer. Man is a being whose Being is the source of his creativity and singularity as man. *Dasein,* human reality or existence, is that structure in which man is disposed to himself as Man. He is neither explained economically, rationally, nor politically; his meaning lies in the ontological structure of his reality.

In this essay of Heidegger the attempt is made to explain how an approach to philosophy is possible. Can philosophy be approached in the same manner as historiography or biology? Heidegger would say no.

Philosophy demands a receptivity or disposition, although not only a receptivity, but the being in the state of receptivity. It requires not only a passive but an active state. Philosophy is listened to; it speaks to man. Philosophy is therefore the dialogue between Being and being, between groundless ground and man. The pre-Socratics were such philosophers, and here in particular Heidegger refers to Heraclitus and Parmenides, because their very language revealed the revealing philosophical realities. Today language has departed from its task of revealing and tries only to represent and classify. The poet, Sophocles or Hölderlin, is a revealer of reality because his language captures the Being of being. The poet's language, as in the case of Hölderlin and Sophocles, allows the Being of being to appear and manifest itself. Thus man listens to philosophy because philosophy is concerned with Being and Being is the reality and structure of being.

When philosophy with Aristotle and Plato turned from Being to being as the fundamental question of metaphysics, according to Heidegger they divided

and estranged Being from being.[3] This for Heidegger was a decisive moment in the history of philosophy. This concern for being was continued in the Middle Ages and through to Nietzsche. The Platonic separation of a world of Ideas and a world of opinion opened the gap between Being and being and destroyed the fundamental ontological inseparability of the Being of being. For Heidegger the pre-Socratics represent the most significant historical philosophical period while Plato and Aristotle manifest a decline when we

3. Heidegger's interpretation of Plato and Aristotle implies a misunderstanding of the position of both. If, for Heidegger, the pre-Socratics had discovered the meaning of metaphysical freedom, it was Plato who realized that this freedom alone was not adequate. For its fulfillment, metaphysical freedom required its concrete manifestation in political and social structures in terms of justice. In the Protagoras myth Plato shows that the freedom of man depends upon the political order and that without reverence and justice man destroys himself. The Platonic position is the necessary other to that of the pre-Socratics. Social, political, and economic life fulfill and make possible metaphysical freedom. Plato and Aristotle provide the necessary other to metaphysical freedom, but in so doing they made it possible for Descartes and modern philosophy to confine itself to the world as representation and idea and lose the metaphysical ground of freedom.

affirm the ontological question of the nature of Being to be the fundamental one.

Rooted so deeply in the pre-Socratic mystery and steeped in German Pietism, the thought of Heidegger becomes strange and difficult to comprehend. We understand so little of this German tradition that when its roots give forth in thought and contemplation we are startled by its novelty and peculiarity. But it is not only to Pietism that we must return to grasp Heidegger but also to his immediate predecessors. Simmel, Scheler, and above all Husserl[4] are fundamental stepping stones for a comprehension of Heidegger. (It should be noted that Heidegger was Husserl's successor in philosophy at Freiburg.)

Heidegger has stated that his position in philosophy is radically different from that of his contemporaries, Sartre and Jaspers. The difference lies in Heidegger's concept of freedom and place and in his definition of humanism. That man *is*, is his freedom. Freedom is rooted in Being and is constituative of being. Free-

---

4. All these philosophers will be considered in our forth-coming volume, *The Search for Being.*

dom is the truth of the human reality. Man "being here" is free because the "being here" reveals the holiness of place, and place is that which permits man to be Man. The loss of place is death.[5] Having a place is the possibility to be some-thing and not no-thing. Place is that reality in which man becomes conscious of himself. It is his ground of existence and the possibility of his realization.

The formal definition of place is completed, however, only in such concrete spheres as the political, economic, and social in which man's place is realized. Each one of these spheres is necessary for the actualization of freedom. Metaphysical freedom is not enough. Heidegger's failure to include a study of the concrete dimensions of freedom in either the economic, social, or political aspects of existence repre-

---

5. This was already revealed in the *Oedipus* of Sophocles and of Seneca. The undeniable right of place is again stated by Antigone (Sophocles) when she demanded that the right to bury her brother transcended the law of the State. Place preceded all other realities. Thomas Hobbes, in his advocacy of absolutism, saw the inviolable nature of place when he stated that the king could not force a man voluntarily to surrender his life.

sents a serious limitation to the full understanding of the dialectical relationship between these and the metaphysical. When we say that man is a political being, we understand that the preservation of political freedom is the realization and confirmation of metaphysical freedom. Nevertheless, the affirmation of metaphysical freedom prevents the adjective, political, from absorbing the substantive, man. The relation between the adjective and the noun must be dialectical. The adjective can not replace the noun nor can the noun realize itself apart from the adjective. The meaning of each is posited by the limits of the other.

The slavery of man results from the fact that the adjective, be it political or economic, has been allowed to absorb within itself the human reality; in this way, it becomes daemonic. Marxism is daemonic, and thus destructive, because the adjective, economic, has absorbed within itself the noun, man. Slavery is the result. Heidegger's position is an heroic attempt to preserve ontological freedom from such daemonic distortions. Heidegger has pointed to the ground of

human freedom, but he fails to show that this ground is achieved or realized only dialectically in opposition to and in reconciliation with the adjective structures of human existence. There can be no metaphysical freedom without political, social, or economic freedom; on the other hand, these concrete freedoms exist only by virtue of metaphysical freedom. Either reality, in and for itself, is destructive. Heidegger has shown the way to a new humanism rooted in the Being of being, but this humanism must relate itself to the structure of human freedom worked out in the political, social, and economic framework. What must be united is the depth of Heidegger's ontology with Mill's or Jefferson's political wisdom.

Heidegger has yet to be completely understood and his place in the framework of European thought has still to be evaluated. That he is the most significant contemporary European philosopher can not be doubted. His concern with the Being of being is a reflection of his deep longing to understand this being we call man and that understanding demands rejection of such definition as rational, economic, or prag-

matic. That Heidegger's approach is religious and poetical, that Böhme, Hölderlin, Heraclitus, or Hebel are his inspiration, does not free us from the responsibility to dispose ourselves to his thinking, comprehend his dimensions, and grasp his questioning. Heidegger struggles with the question which each man must struggle with—what is the meaning of *Dasein* or the human reality? The question, and its possible answer, is the responsibility of all philosophy. Heidegger has posed the question and he has pointed a path where an awareness of Being is to be found. They are new dimensions for us and in these dimensions the limitations of our own traditions are loosened and we are led to deeper questioning. This reaffirmation of the very nature of philosophy is the unique and original achievement of Martin Heidegger.

Among the most important works of Heidegger, *Sein und Zeit* (1927) remains fundamental. Much of Heidegger's philosophical production has been in the form of lectures which were later published.[6] It

6. *Was ist das—die Philosophie?* was a lecture given in Cérisy-la-Salle, Normandy, in August 1955.

has often been suggested that *Was ist Metaphysik?* (1929) is the best introduction to Heidegger. This work has led to such confused and unintelligent criticism of Heidegger that one would probably get a better preliminary understanding from the essay we are presenting here, followed by the first section of *Sein und Zeit*. Perhaps the clearest and most precise presentation of Heidegger's thought lies in his *Einführung in die Metaphysik* (1935). His most traditional philosophic work remains *Kant und das Problem der Metaphysik* (1929). The complete opus of Heidegger remains as yet small although additional volumes dealing with varied aspects of philosophy and philosophies are to be published.

Our translation is offered only as a guide to the reading of the German text. Heidegger's thought can not be reproduced in any other language. We hope that in offering the translation we do not create the idea that we are presenting a substitute for the German text; we present only a vehicle for its comprehension.

Qu'est- ce que la philosophie?

Was ist das – die Philosophie?

Mit dieser Frage rühren wir an ein Thema, das sehr weit, d. h. ausgedehnt ist. Weil das Thema weit ist, bleibt es unbestimmt. Weil es unbestimmt ist, können wir das Thema unter den verschiedenartigsten Gesichtspunkten behandeln. Dabei werden wir immer etwas Richtiges treffen. Weil jedoch bei der Behandlung dieses weitläufigen Themas alle nur möglichen Ansichten durcheinanderlaufen, kommen wir in die Gefahr, daß unser Gespräch ohne die rechte Sammlung bleibt.

Darum müssen wir versuchen, die Frage genauer zu bestimmen. Auf solche Weise bringen wir das Gespräch in eine feste Richtung. Das Gespräch wird dadurch auf

18

WHAT IS PHILOSOPHY?

With this question we are touching on a theme which is very broad, that is, widespread. Because the theme is broad, it is indefinite. Because it is indefinite, we can treat the theme from the most varied points of view. Thereby we shall always hit upon something that is valid. But because, in the treatment of this extensive theme, all possible opinions intermingle, we are in danger of having our discussion lack proper cohesion.

Therefore, we must try to define the question more exactly. In this manner we direct the discussion into a definite direction. The discussion is thereby brought

einen Weg gebracht. Ich sage: auf *einen* Weg. Damit geben wir zu, daß dieser Weg gewiß nicht der einzige Weg ist. Es muß sogar offen bleiben, ob der Weg, auf den ich im folgenden hinweisen möchte, in Wahrheit ein Weg ist, der uns erlaubt, die Frage zu stellen und zu beantworten.

Nehmen wir einmal an, wir könnten einen Weg finden, die Frage genauer zu bestimmen, dann erhebt sich sogleich ein schwerwiegender Einwand gegen das Thema unseres Gespräches. Wenn wir fragen: Was ist das – die Philosophie?, dann sprechen wir *über* die Philosophie. Indem wir auf diese Weise fragen, bleiben wir offenbar auf einem Standort oberhalb und d. h. außerhalb der Philosophie. Aber das Ziel unserer Frage ist, *in* die Philosophie hineinzukommen, in ihr uns aufzuhalten, nach ihrer Weise uns zu verhalten, d. h. zu „philosophieren". Der Weg unserer Gespräche muß deshalb nicht nur eine klare Richtung haben, sondern diese Richtung muß uns zugleich auch die Gewähr bieten, daß wir uns innerhalb der Philosophie bewegen und nicht außen um sie herum.

into a path. I say—into *a* path. Thereby we admit that this path is certainly not the only one. It must, in fact, remain open whether the path which I should like to indicate in what follows is, in truth, a path which allows us to pose and answer the question.

If we now assume that we might find a way of determining the question more exactly, then there immediately arises a grave objection to the theme of our discussion. When we ask, "What is philosophy?" then we are speaking *about* philosophy. By asking in this way we are obviously taking a stand above and, therefore, outside of philosophy. But the aim of our question is to enter *into* philosophy, to tarry in it, to conduct ourselves in its manner, that is, to "philosophize." The path of our discussion must, therefore, not only have a clear direction, but this direction must at the same time give us the guarantee that we are moving within philosophy and not outside of it and around it.

Der Weg unserer Gespräche muß also von einer Art und Richtung sein, daß das, wovon die Philosophie handelt, uns selbst angeht, uns berührt (nous touche), und zwar uns in unserem Wesen.

Aber wird die Philosophie dadurch nicht zu einer Sache der Affektion, der Affekte und der Gefühle?

„Mit den schönen Gefühlen macht man die schlechte Literatur." „C'est avec les beaux sentiments que l'on fait la mauvaise littérature."* Dieses Wort von André Gide gilt nicht nur von der Literatur, es gilt mehr noch für die Philosophie. Gefühle, auch die schönsten, gehören nicht in die Philosophie. Gefühle, sagt man, sind etwas Irrationales. Die Philosophie dagegen ist nicht nur etwas Rationales, sondern die eigentliche Verwalterin der Ratio. Indem wir dies behaupten, haben wir unversehens etwas darüber entschieden, was die Philosophie ist. Wir sind unserer Frage mit einer Antwort schon vorausgeeilt. Jedermann hält die Aussage, daß die Philosophie eine Sache der Ratio sei, für richtig. Vielleicht ist diese Aussage den-

* André Gide. Dostoïewsky. Paris 1923; p. 247.

22

The path of our discussion must, therefore, be of such a kind and direction that that of which philosophy treats concerns us personally, affects us and, indeed, touches us in our very nature.

But does not philosophy thereby become a matter of affection, emotions, and sentiments?

"With fine sentiments bad literature is made."[1] These words of André Gide apply not only to literature but even more to philosophy. Sentiments, even the finest, have no place in philosophy. Sentiments, it is said, are something irrational. Philosophy, on the other hand, is not only something rational but is the actual guardian of reason. In making this assertion we have come unawares to a kind of decision as to what philosophy is. We have already anticipated our question with an answer. Everyone considers the assertion correct that philosophy is a matter of reason. How-

1. André Gide, *Dostoievsky* (Paris: Plon-Nourrit, 1923), p. 247.

noch eine voreilige und überstürzte Antwort auf die Frage : Was ist das – die Philosophie? Denn wir können dieser Antwort sogleich neue Fragen entgegensetzen. Was ist das – die Ratio, die Vernunft? Wo und durch wen wurde entschieden, was die Ratio ist? Hat sich die Ratio selbst zur Herrin der Philosophie gemacht? Wenn „ja", mit welchem Recht? Wenn „nein", woher empfängt sie ihren Auftrag und ihre Rolle? Wenn das, was als Ratio gilt, erst und nur durch die Philosophie und innerhalb des Ganges ihrer Geschichte festgelegt wurde, dann ist es kein guter Rat, die Philosophie zum voraus als Sache der Ratio auszugeben. Sobald wir jedoch die Kennzeichnung der Philosophie als eines rationalen Verhaltens in Zweifel ziehen, wird in gleicher Weise auch bezweifelbar, ob die Philosophie in den Bereich des Irrationalen gehöre. Denn wer die Philosophie als irrational bestimmen will, nimmt dabei das Rationale zum Maßstab der Abgrenzung und zwar in einer Weise, daß er wiederum als selbstverständlich voraussetzt, was die Ratio ist. Wenn wir andererseits auf die Möglichkeit hinweisen,

ever, this assertion is perhaps a premature and hasty answer to the question, "What is philosophy?" for we can immediately oppose new questions to this answer. What is reason? Where and through whom was it decided what reason is? Has reason constituted itself to be the ruler of philosophy? If so, by what right? If not, whence does it obtain its mission and its role? If what is considered to be reason was first established only by philosophy and within the course of its history, then it is not good judgment to proclaim philosophy in advance as a matter of reason. However, as soon as we cast doubt on the characterization of philosophy as rational behavior, then in the same way it also becomes questionable whether philosophy belongs in the domain of the irrational. For whoever wishes to designate philosophy as irrational thereby takes the rational as a measure of limitation and, what is more, does it in such a way as again to take for granted what reason is.

If, on the other hand, we point out the possibility

daß das, worauf die Philosophie sich bezieht, uns Menschen in unserem Wesen angeht und uns be-rührt, dann könnte es sein, daß diese Affektion durchaus nichts mit dem zu tun hat, was man gewöhnlich Affekte und Gefühle, kurz das Irrationale nennt.

Aus dem Gesagten entnehmen wir zunächst nur dieses eine: Es bedarf einer höheren Sorgfalt, wenn wir es wagen, ein Gespräch unter dem Titel „Was ist das – die Philosophie?" zu beginnen.

Das erste ist, daß wir versuchen, die Frage auf einen klar gerichteten Weg zu bringen, damit wir nicht in beliebigen und nicht in zufälligen Vorstellungen über die Philosophie umhertreiben. Doch wie sollen wir einen Weg finden, auf dem wir in einer zuverlässigen Weise unsere Frage bestimmen?

Der Weg, auf den ich jetzt hinweisen möchte, liegt unmittelbar vor uns. Und nur deshalb, weil er der nächstliegende ist, finden wir ihn schwer. Wenn wir ihn aber gefunden haben, dann bewegen wir uns trotzdem immer noch unbeholfen auf ihm. Wir fragen: Was ist das – die

that that upon which philosophy bears concerns us humans in our essential nature and moves[2] us, then it might be that this being-moved has nothing whatsoever to do with that which is usually called feelings and emotions, in short, the irrational.

From what has been said, we deduce at first only this one thing: greater care is required if we hazard a discussion under the title "What is Philosophy?"

The first thing for us to do is to lead the question to a clearly directed path so that we do not flounder around in either convenient or haphazard conceptions of philosophy. But how are we to find a path by which we can determine our question reliably?

The path which I should now like to point out lies directly before us. And only because it is the nearest at hand is it difficult to find. However, when we have found it, we still move along it awkwardly. We ask,

2. *be-rühren*, as Heidegger uses it here, indicates not an emotional stirring but a metaphysical stirring, consequently, not an affection but an essential movement.

Philosophie? Wir haben das Wort „Philosophie" schon oft genug ausgesprochen. Wenn wir aber das Wort „Philosophie" jetzt nicht mehr wie einen abgebrauchten Titel verwenden, wenn wir statt dessen das Wort „Philosophie" aus seinem Ursprung hören, dann lautet es: φιλοσοφία. Das Wort „Philosophie" spricht jetzt griechisch. Das griechische Wort ist als *griechisches* Wort ein Weg. Dieser liegt einerseits vor uns, denn das Wort ist uns seit langer Zeit vorausgesprochen. Andererseits liegt er schon hinter uns, denn wir haben dieses Wort immer schon gehört und gesagt. Demgemäß ist das griechische Wort φιλοσοφία ein Weg, auf dem wir unterwegs sind. Doch wir kennen diesen Weg nur ganz undeutlich, obwohl wir viele historische Kenntnisse über die griechische Philosophie besitzen und ausbreiten können.

Das Wort φιλοσοφία sagt uns, daß die Philosophie etwas ist, was erstmals die Existenz des Griechentums bestimmt. Nicht nur das – die φιλοσοφία bestimmt auch den innersten Grundzug unserer abendländisch - europäischen

"What is philosophy?" We have uttered the word "philosophy" often enough. If, however, we use the word "philosophy" no longer like a wornout title, if, instead, we hear the word "philosophy" coming from its source, then it sounds thus: *philosophia*. Now the word "philosophy" is speaking Greek. The word, as a Greek word, is a path. This path, on the one hand, lies before us, for the word has long since been spoken, i.e. set forth. On the other hand, it lies behind us, for we have always heard and spoken this word. Accordingly, the Greek word *philosophia* is a path along which we are traveling. Yet we have only a vague knowledge of this path although we possess and can spread much historical information about Greek philosophy.

The word *philosophia* tells us that philosophy is something which, first of all, determines the existence of the Greek world. Not only that—*philosophia* also determines the innermost basic feature of our Western-European history. The often heard expression

Geschichte. Die oft gehörte Redeweise von der „abendländisch-europäischen Philosophie" ist in Wahrheit eine Tautologie. Warum? Weil die „Philosophie" in ihrem Wesen griechisch ist –, griechisch heißt hier: die Philosophie ist im Ursprung ihres Wesens von der Art, daß sie zuerst das Griechentum, und nur dieses, in Anspruch genommen hat, um sich zu entfalten.

Allein – das ursprünglich griechische Wesen der Philosophie wird in der Epoche seines neuzeitlich-europäischen Waltens von Vorstellungen des Christentums geleitet und beherrscht. Die Herrschaft dieser Vorstellungen ist durch das Mittelalter vermittelt. Gleichwohl kann man nicht sagen, die Philosophie werde dadurch christlich, d. h. zu einer Sache des Glaubens an die Offenbarung und die Autorität der Kirche. Der Satz: die Philosophie ist in ihrem Wesen griechisch, sagt nichts anderes als: das Abendland und Europa, und nur sie, sind in ihrem innersten Geschichtsgang ursprünglich „philosophisch". Das wird durch die Entstehung und Herrschaft der Wissenschaften bezeugt. Weil sie dem innersten abend-

"Western-European philosophy" is, in truth, a tautology. Why? Because philosophy is Greek in its nature; Greek, in this instance, means that in origin the nature of philosophy is of such a kind that it first appropriated the Greek world, and only it, in order to unfold.

However, the originally Greek nature of philosophy, in the era of its modern-European sway, has been guided and ruled by Christian conceptions. The dominance of these conceptions was mediated by the Middle Ages. At the same time, one cannot say that philosophy thereby became Christian, that is, became a matter of belief in revelation and the authority of the Church. The statement that philosophy is in its nature Greek says nothing more than that the West and Europe, and only these, are, in the innermost course of their history, originally "philosophical." This is attested by the rise and dominance of the sciences. Because they stem from the innermost Western-Euro-

31

ländisch-europäischen Geschichtsgang, nämlich dem
philosophischen entstammen, deshalb sind sie heute imstande, der Geschichte des Menschen auf der ganzen
Erde die spezifische Prägung zu geben.

Überlegen wir uns einen Augenblick, was es bedeutet, daß
man ein Weltalter der Menschengeschichte als „Atomzeitalter" kennzeichnet. Die durch die Wissenschaften
entdeckte und freigesetzte Atomenergie wird als diejenige Macht vorgestellt, die den Geschichtsgang bestimmen soll. Die Wissenschaften gäbe es freilich niemals,
wenn ihnen nicht die Philosophie vorher- und vorausge-
gangen wäre. Die Philosophie aber ist : ἡ φιλοσοφία. Dieses
griechische Wort bindet unser Gespräch in eine geschichtliche Überlieferung. Weil diese Überlieferung einzigartig
bleibt, deshalb ist sie auch eindeutig. Die durch den griechischen Namen φιλοσοφία genannte Überlieferung, die
uns das geschichtliche Wort φιλοσοφία nennt, gibt uns
die Richtung eines Weges frei, auf dem wir fragen : Was
ist das – die Philosophie? Die Überlieferung liefert uns
nicht einem Zwang des Vergangenen und Unwiderruf-

pean course of history, that is, the philosophical, consequently they are able, today, to put a specific imprint on the history of mankind upon the whole earth.

Let us consider for a moment what it means that an era in the history of mankind is characterized as the "atomic age." The atomic energy discovered and liberated by the sciences is represented as that force which is to determine the course of history. Indeed, there would never have been any sciences if philosophy had not preceded them and proceeded. But philosophy is *the philosophia*. This Greek word binds our discussion to an historical tradition. Because this tradition is of a unique kind, it is also unique in meaning. This tradition which bears the Greek name *philosophia*, and which is labelled for us with the historical word *philosophia*, reveals the direction of a path on which we ask, "What is philosophy?" Tradition does not surrender us to a constraint by what is past and

lichen aus. Überliefern, délivrer, ist ein Befreien, nämlich in die Freiheit des Gespräches mit dem Gewesenen.
Der Name „Philosophie" ruft uns, wenn wir das Wort
wahrhaft hören und das Gehörte bedenken, in die Geschichte der griechischen Herkunft der Philosophie. Das
Wort φιλοσοφία steht gleichsam auf der Geburtsurkunde
unserer eigenen Geschichte, wir dürfen sogar sagen:
auf der Geburtsurkunde der gegenwärtigen weltge-
schichtlichen Epoche, die sich Atomzeitalter nennt.
Darum können wir die Frage: Was ist das – die Philosophie? nur fragen, wenn wir uns in ein Gespräch mit
dem Denken des Griechentums einlassen.

Aber nicht allein dasjenige, *was* in Frage steht, die Philosophie, ist seiner Herkunft nach griechisch, sondern
auch die Weise, *wie* wir fragen; die Weise, in der wir
auch heute noch fragen, ist griechisch.

Wir fragen: was ist das . . .? Dies lautet griechisch: τί
ἐστιν. Die Frage, was etwas sei, bleibt jedoch mehrdeu-
tig. Wir können fragen: was ist das dort in der Ferne?
Wir erhalten die Antwort: ein Baum. Die Antwort

34

irrevocable. Surrendering is a delivering into the freedom of discussion with what has been. If we truly
hear the word and reflect upon what we have heard,
the name "philosophy" summons us into the history
of the Greek origin of philosophy. The word *philosophia* appears, as it were, on the birth eertificate of
our own history; we may even say on the birth cer-
tificate of the contemporary epoch of world history
which is called the atomic age. That is why we can
ask the question, "What is philosophy?" only if we
enter into a discussion with the thinking of the Greek
world.

But not only *what* is in question—philosophy—is
Greek in origin, but *how* we question, the manner in
which we question even today, is Greek.

We ask, "what is that?" In Greek this sounds *ti estin*
[what is it?]. The question of *what* something is, however, has more than one meaning. We can ask, "what
is that over there in the distance?" We receive the
answer, "a tree." The answer consists in the fact that

besteht darin, daß wir einem Ding, das wir nicht genau erkennen, seinen Namen geben.

Wir können jedoch weiter fragen: Was ist das, was wir „Baum" nennen? Mit der jetzt gestellten Frage kommen wir schon in die Nähe des griechischen τί ἐστιν. Es ist diejenige Form des Fragens, die Sokrates, Platon und Aristoteles entfaltet haben. Sie fragen z. B.: Was ist dies – das Schöne? Was ist dies – die Erkenntnis? Was ist dies – die Natur? Was ist dies – die Bewegung?

Nun müssen wir aber darauf achten, daß in den soeben genannten Fragen nicht nur eine genauere Umgrenzung dessen gesucht wird, was Natur, was Bewegung, was Schönheit ist, sondern: daß auch zugleich eine Auslegung darüber gegeben wird, was das „Was" bedeutet, in welchem Sinne das τί zu verstehen ist. Man nennt dasjenige, was das Was bedeutet, das quid est, τὸ quid: die quidditas, die Washeit. Indessen wird die quidditas in den verschiedenen Epochen der Philosophie verschieden bestimmt. So ist z. B. die Philosophie Platons eine eigenartige Interpretation dessen, was das τί meint. Es meint

we name a thing which we do not clearly recognize.

We can, however, ask further, "what is that which we call a 'tree'?" With the question now posited we are already approaching the Greek *ti estin* [what is it?]. It is this form of questioning which Socrates, Plato, and Aristotle developed. They ask, for example, "What is the beautiful? What is knowledge? What is Nature? What is movement?"

Now we must, however, be careful that in the questions just mentioned not only a more exact delimitation is sought of what Nature, movement, or beauty is, but also that, at the same time, an interpretation is given of what the "what" means, in what sense the *ti* [what] is to be understood. That which "what" means is called the *quid est, to* [the] *quid,* the quiddity, the whatness. However, the quiddity is determined differently in the various periods of philosophy. Thus, for example, the philosophy of Plato is a specific interpretation of what the what signifies, namely the *idea*.

nämlich die Ἰδέα. Daß wir, wenn wir nach dem τί, nach dem quid fragen, dabei die „Idea" meinen, ist keineswegs selbstverständlich. Aristoteles gibt eine andere Auslegung des τί als Platon. Eine andere Auslegung des τί gibt Kant, eine andere Hegel. Was am Leitfaden des τί, des quid, des Was jeweils gefragt ist, bleibt jedesmal neu zu bestimmen. In jedem Falle gilt: wenn wir in bezug auf die Philosophie fragen: Was ist das?, dann fragen wir eine ursprünglich griechische Frage.

Beachten wir es gut: sowohl das Thema unserer Frage: „die Philosophie", als auch die Weise, in der wir fragen: „was ist das...?" – beides bleibt seiner Herkunft nach griechisch. Wir selbst gehören in diese Herkunft, auch dann, wenn wir das Wort „Philosophie" nicht einmal nennen. Wir sind eigens in diese Herkunft zurückgerufen, für sie und durch sie re-klamiert, sobald wir die Frage: Was ist das – die Philosophie? nicht nur in ihrem Wortlaut aussprechen, sondern ihrem Sinne nachsinnen. [Die Frage: Was ist Philosophie? ist keine Frage, die eine Art von Erkenntnis an sich selbst richtet (Philosophie der

That we mean the *idea* when we ask about the *ti* and and the *quid* is by no means to be taken as a matter of course. Aristotle gives an interpretation of the *ti* different from that of Plato. Kant gives another interpretation of the *ti*, Hegel still another. That which is asked each time by means of the clues of the *ti*, the *quid*, the "what," is to be newly determined each time. In every case when, in regard to philosophy, we ask, "what is that?" then we are asking an originally Greek question.

Let us bear well in mind that both the theme of our question—"philosophy"—as well as the way in which we ask "what is that . . . ?" are Greek in origin. We ourselves belong to this origin even when we do not mention the word "philosophy." We are peculiarly summoned back into this source and are re-claimed for and by it as soon as we not only utter the words of the question, "What is philosophy?" but reflect upon its meaning. [The question, "What is philosophy?" is not a question which directs a kind of

Philosophie). Die Frage ist auch keine historische Frage, die sich dafür interessiert auszumachen, wie das, was man „Philosophie" nennt, begonnen und sich entwickelt hat. Die Frage ist eine geschichtliche, d. h. geschick-liche Frage. Mehr noch: sie ist nicht „eine", sie ist *die* geschichtliche Frage unseres abendländisch-europäischen Daseins.]

Wenn wir auf den ganzen und ursprünglichen Sinn der Frage: Was ist das – die Philosophie? uns einlassen, dann hat unser Fragen durch seine geschichtliche Herkunft eine Richtung in eine geschichtliche Zukunft gefunden. Wir haben einen Weg gefunden. Die Frage selbst ist ein Weg. Er führt von dem Dasein des Griechentums her zu uns hin, wenn nicht gar über uns hinaus. Wir sind – wenn wir bei der Frage ausharren – unterwegs auf einem klar gerichteten Weg. Dennoch haben wir dadurch noch keine Gewähr, daß wir unmittelbar imstande sind, diesen Weg auf die rechte Weise zu gehen. Wir können nicht einmal sogleich ausmachen, an welcher Stelle des Weges wir heute stehen. Man pflegt seit

knowledge towards itself (philosophy of philosophy).
Nor is it an historical question which is interested in
determining how that which is called "philosophy"
began and developed. The question is an historical,
that means, a fate-full question. Even more—it is not
a it is *the* historical question of our Western-European
actuality.]

If we enter into the total and original meaning of
the question, "What is philosophy?" then our questioning has, through its historical origin, found a
direction into an historical future. We have found a
path. The question itself is a path. It leads from the
actuality of the Greek world down to us, if not, indeed, beyond us. We are—if we persist in this question
—traveling on a clearly indicated path. Nevertheless,
we still have no guarantee thereby that we are immediately enabled to pursue this path in the right way.
We cannot even determine at once at which point on
this path we are standing today. For a long time

langer Zeit die Frage, was etwas sei, als die Frage nach dem Wesen zu kennzeichnen. Die Frage nach dem Wesen wird jeweils dann wach, wenn dasjenige, nach dessen Wesen gefragt wird, sich verdunkelt und verwirrt hat, wenn zugleich der Bezug des Menschen zu dem Befragten schwankend geworden oder gar erschüttert ist.

Die Frage unseres Gespräches betrifft das Wesen der Philosophie. Wenn diese Frage aus einer Not kommt und nicht bloß eine Scheinfrage zum Zweck einer Konversation bleiben soll, dann muß uns die Philosophie als Philosophie fragwürdig geworden sein. Trifft dies zu? Und wenn ja, inwiefern ist die Philosophie für uns fragwürdig geworden? Dies können wir offenbar doch nur dann angeben, wenn wir schon einen Einblick in die Philosophie genommen haben. Dazu ist nötig, daß wir zuvor wissen, was das ist – die Philosophie. So werden wir auf eine seltsame Weise in einem Kreis herumgejagt. Die Philosophie selbst scheint dieser Kreis zu sein. Angenommen, wir könnten uns aus dem Ring dieses Kreises nicht unmittelbar befreien, so ist uns doch erlaubt, auf den Kreis

we have been accustomed to characterize the question of what something is as a question about its nature. The question about the nature of something awakens at those times when that, whose nature is being questioned, has become obscure and confused, when at the same time the relationship of men to what is being questioned has become uncertain or has even been shattered.

The question of our discussion concerns the nature of philosophy. If this question arises from a need and is not to remain only a hypothetical question for the purpose of making conversation, then philosophy as philosophy must have become worthy of question. Obviously we can indicate this only if we have already taken a look into philosophy. In order to do this we must know beforehand what philosophy is. Thus, in a strange manner, we are being chased around in a circle. Philosophy itself seems to be this circle. Assuming that we might not be able to escape immediately out of the ring of this circle, we still are per-

zu blicken. Wohin soll sich unser Blick wenden? Das griechische Wort φιλοσοφία weist uns die Richtung.

Hier ist eine grundsätzliche Bemerkung nötig. Wenn wir jetzt und später auf Worte der griechischen Sprache hören, dann begeben wir uns in einen ausgezeichneten Bereich. Langsam dämmert nämlich für unsere Besinnung, daß die griechische Sprache keine bloße Sprache ist wie die uns bekannten europäischen Sprachen. Die griechische Sprache, und sie allein, ist λόγος. Wir werden in unseren Gesprächen davon noch eingehender handeln müssen. Für den Beginn genüge der Hinweis, daß in der griechischen Sprache das in ihr Gesagte auf eine ausgezeichnete Weise zugleich das ist, was das Gesagte nennt. Wenn wir ein griechisches Wort griechisch hören, dann folgen wir seinem λέγειν, seinem unmittelbaren Darlegen. Was es darlegt, ist das Vorliegende. Wir sind durch das griechisch gehörte Wort unmittelbar bei der vorliegenden Sache selbst, nicht zunächst bei einer bloßen Wortbedeutung.

Das griechische Wort φιλοσοφία geht auf das Wort φιλό-

mitted to look at the circle. In which direction should our glance turn? The Greek word *philosophia* indicates the direction.

Here a statement of principle is required. If we listen now and later to the words of the Greek language, then we move into a distinct and distinguished domain. Slowly it will dawn upon our thinking that the Greek language is no mere language like the European languages known to us. The Greek language, and it alone, is *logos*. We shall have to deal with this in greater detail in our discussions. For the time being let it be sufficient to suggest that in the Greek language what is said in it *is* at the same time in an excellent way what it is called. If we hear a Greek word with a Greek ear we follow its *legein* [its speaking], its direct presentation. What it presents is what lies immediately before us. Through the audible Greek word we are directly in the presence of the thing itself, not first in the presence of a mere word sign.

The Greek word *philosophia* goes back to the word

σοφος zurück. Dieses Wort ist ursprünglich ein Adiectivum wie φιλάργυρος, silberliebend, wie φιλότιμος, ehrliebend. Das Wort φιλόσοφος wurde vermutlich von Heraklit geprägt. Dies besagt: für Heraklit gibt es noch nicht die φιλοσοφία. Ein ἀνήρ φιλόσοφος ist nicht ein „philosophischer" Mensch. Das griechische Adiectivum φιλόσοφος sagt etwas völlig anderes als die Adiectiva philosophisch, philosophique. Ein ἀνήρ φιλόσοφος ist derjenige, ὅς φιλεῖ τὸ σοφόν, der das σοφόν liebt; φιλεῖν, lieben bedeutet hier im Sinne Heraklits: ὁμολογεῖν, so sprechen, wie der Λόγος spricht, d. h. dem Λόγος entsprechen. Dieses Entsprechen steht im Einklang mit dem σοφόν. Einklang ist ἁρμονία. Dies, daß ein Wesen dem anderen wechselweise sich fügt, daß sich beide ursprünglich einander fügen, weil sie zueinander verfügt sind, diese ἁρμονία ist das Auszeichnende des heraklitisch gedachten φιλεῖν, des Liebens.

Der ἀνήρ φιλόσοφος liebt das σοφόν. Was dieses Wort für Heraklit sagt, ist schwer zu übersetzen. Aber wir können es nach Heraklits eigener Auslegung erläutern. Dem-

philosophos. This word is originally an adjective like *philarguros,* loving silver, like *philotomos,* loving honor. The word *philosophos* was presumably coined by Heraclitus. This indicates that for Heraclitus *philosophia* did not yet exist. An *aner philosophos* is not a "philosophical" man. The Greek adjective *philosophos* expresses something completely different from the adjective philosophical. An *aner philosophos* is *hos philei to sophon,* he who loves the *sophon; philein,* to love, signifies here, in the Heraclitean sense, *homolegein,* to speak in the way in which the *Logos* speaks, in correspondence with the *Logos.*[3] This correspondence is in accord with the *sophon.* Accordance is *harmonia.* That one being reciprocally unites itself with another, that both are originally united to each other because they are at each other's disposal—this *harmonia* is the distinctive feature of *philein,* of "loving" in the Heraclitean sense.

The *aner philosophos* loves the *sophon.* What this word means for Heraclitus is hard to translate. But we can explain it according to Heraclitus' own interpreta-

3. The use of the words *sprechen* and *entsprechen* indicates the inner dialectic which exists in the structure of speaking itself. Speaking—to be speaking—requires correspondence.

nach sagt τὸ σοφόν dieses: Ἕν Πάντα, „Eines (ist) Alles".
„Alles", das meint hier: Πάντα τὰ ὄντα, das Ganze, das
All des Seienden. Ἕν, das Eins meint: das Eine, Einzige,
alles Einigende. Einig aber ist alles Seiende im Sein. Das
σοφόν sagt: Alles Seiende ist im Sein. Schärfer gesagt:
Das Sein *ist* das Seiende. Hierbei spricht „ist" transitiv
und besagt soviel wie „versammelt". Das Sein versammelt das Seiende darin, daß es Seiendes ist. Das Sein ist
die Versammlung – Λόγος.*

Alles Seiende ist im Sein. Solches zu hören, klingt für
unser Ohr trivial, wenn nicht gar beleidigend. Denn
darum, daß das Seiende in das Sein gehört, braucht sich
niemand zu kümmern. Alle Welt weiß: Seiendes ist solches, was ist. Was steht dem Seienden anderes frei als
dies: zu sein? Und dennoch: gerade dies, daß das Seiende
im Sein versammelt bleibt, daß im Scheinen von Sein
das Seiende erscheint, dies setzte die Griechen, und sie
zuerst und sie allein, in das Erstaunen. Seiendes im Sein:
dies wurde für die Griechen das Erstaunlichste.

* vgl. Vorträge und Aufsätze. 1954, Seite 207–229.

tion. According to this the *sophon* means, *Hen Panta*, "One (is) all." "All" means here, all things that exist, the whole, the totality of being. *Hen*, one, means, the one, the unique, the all-uniting. But all being is united in Being. The *sophon* says—all being is in Being. To put it more pointedly—being *is* Being. In this instance "is" speaks transitively and means approximately "gathered together," "collected." Being gathers being together in so far as it is being. Being is the gathering together—*Logos*.[4]

All being is in Being. To hear such a thing sounds trivial to our ear, if not, indeed, offensive, for no one needs to bother about the fact that being belongs in Being. All the world knows that being is that which is. What else remains for being but to be? And yet, just this fact that being is gathered together in Being, that in the appearance of Being being appears, that astonished the Greeks and first astonished them and them alone. Being [small "b"] in Being—that became the most astonishing thing for the Greeks.

4. Cf. *Vorträge und Aufsätze*, 1954, pp. 207-229.

Indessen mußten sogar die Griechen die Erstaunlichkeit dieses Erstaunlichsten retten und schützen – gegen den Zugriff des sophistischen Verstandes, der für alles eine für jedermann sogleich verständliche Erklärung bereit hatte und sie auf den Markt brachte. Die Rettung des Erstaunlichsten – Seiendes im Sein – geschah dadurch, daß sich einige auf den Weg machten in der Richtung auf dieses Erstaunlichste, d. h. das σοφόν. Sie wurden dadurch zu solchen, die nach dem σοφόν *strebten* und durch ihr eigenes Streben bei anderen Menschen die Sehnsucht nach dem σοφόν erweckten und wachhielten. Das φιλεῖν τὸ σοφόν, jener schon genannte Einklang mit dem σοφόν, die ἁρμονία, wurde so zu einer ὄρεξις, zu einem *Streben* nach dem σοφόν. Das σοφόν – das Seiende im Sein – wird jetzt eigens gesucht. Weil das φιλεῖν nicht mehr ein ursprünglicher Einklang mit dem σοφόν ist, sondern ein besonderes Streben *nach* dem σοφόν, wird das φιλεῖν τὸ σοφόν zur ,,φιλοσοφία''. Deren Streben wird durch den Eros bestimmt.

Dieses strebende Suchen nach dem σοφόν, nach dem Ἓν

However, even the Greeks had to rescue and protect the astonishingness of this most astonishing thing against the attack of Sophist reasoning which always had ready for everything an answer which was comprehensible to everyone and which they put on the market. The rescue of the most astonishing thing—being in Being—was accomplished by a few who started off in the direction of this most astonishing thing, that is, the *sophon*. By doing this they became those who *strove* for the *sophon* and who through their own striving awakened and kept alive among others the yearning for the *sophon*. The loving the *sophon*, that already mentioned harmony with the *sophon*, the *harmonia*, thus became an *orexis* [yearning], a *striving* for the *sophon*. The *sophon*—the being in Being—is now especially sought. Because the loving is no longer an original harmony with the *sophon* but is a particular striving *towards* the *sophon*, the loving of the *sophon* becomes *"philosophia."* The striving is determined by Eros.

This yearning search for the *sophon*, for the "One

Πάντα, nach dem Seienden im Sein wird jetzt zur Frage: Was ist das Seiende, insofern es ist? Das Denken wird jetzt erst zur „Philosophie". Heraklit und Parmenides waren noch keine „Philosophen". Warum nicht? Weil sie die größeren Denker waren. „Größer" meint hier nicht das Verrechnen einer Leistung, sondern zeigt in eine andere Dimension des Denkens. Heraklit und Parmenides waren „größer" in dem Sinne, daß sie noch im Einklang standen mit dem Λόγος, d. h. dem Ἕν Πάντα. Der Schritt zur „Philosophie", vorbereitet durch die Sophistik, wurde zuerst von Sokrates und Platon vollzogen. Aristoteles hat dann fast zwei Jahrhunderte nach Heraklit diesen Schritt durch folgenden Satz gekennzeichnet: καὶ δὴ καὶ τὸ πάλαι τε καὶ νῦν καὶ ἀεὶ ζητούμενον καὶ ἀεὶ ἀπορούμενον, τί τὸ ὄν; (Met. Z 1, 1028 b 2 sqq). In der Übersetzung sagt dies: „Und so ist denn einstmals schon und auch jetzt und immerfort dasjenige, wohin (die Philosophie) sich auf den Weg begibt und wohin sie immer wieder den Zugang nicht findet, (das Gefragte dieses): Was ist das Seiende? (τί τὸ ὄν)."

52

(is) all," for the being in Being, now becomes the question, "What is being, in so far as it is?" Only now does thinking become "philosophy." Heraclitus and Parmenides were not yet "philosophers." Why not? Because they were the greater thinkers. "Greater" here does not signify the estimation of an achievement but indicates another dimension of thinking. Heraclitus and Parmenidies were "greater" in the sense that they were still in harmony with the *Logos,* that is, with the "One (is) all." The step into "philosophy," prepared for by Sophism, was first accomplished by Socrates and Plato. Then, almost two centuries after Heraclitus, Aristotle characterized this step by the following statement: "And, moreover, that which is sought both of old and now and forever and forever missed is, what is being." (*Met.* Z 1, 1028 b 2 sqq). In translation this reads: "And thus, as was in the past, is now too and will be ever more, that towards which (philosophy) is moving and to which it again and again does not find access, is (the question raised)— what is being? (*ti to on*)."

Die Philosophie sucht das, was das Seiende ist, insofern es ist. Die Philosophie ist unterwegs zum Sein des Seienden, d. h. zum Seienden hinsichtlich des Seins. Aristoteles erläutert dies, indem er in dem angeführten Satz auf das τί τὸ ὄν, was ist das Seiende? eine Erläuterung folgen läßt: τοῦτό ἐστι τίς ἡ οὐσία; in der Übersetzung gesprochen: „Dies (nämlich τί τὸ ὄν) bedeutet: was ist die Seiendheit des Seienden?" Das Sein des Seienden beruht in der Seiendheit. Diese aber – die οὐσία – bestimmt Platon als ἰδέα, bestimmt Aristoteles als die ἐνέργεια.

Im Augenblick ist es noch nicht nötig, genauer zu erörtern, was Aristoteles mit ἐνέργεια meint und inwiefern sich die οὐσία durch die ἐνέργεια bestimmen läßt. Wichtig ist jetzt nur dies, daß wir darauf achten, wie Aristoteles die Philosophie in ihrem Wesen umgrenzt. Er sagt im ersten Buch der „Metaphysik" (Met. A 2, 982 b 9 sq) folgendes: die Philosophie ist ἐπιστήμη τῶν πρώτων ἀρχῶν καὶ αἰτιῶν θεωρητική. Man übersetzt ἐπιστήμη gern durch „Wissenschaft". Das ist irreführend, weil wir allzuleicht die moderne Vorstellung von „Wissenschaft" einfließen

54

Philosophy seeks what being is, in so far as it is. Philosophy is en route to the Being of being, that is, to being with respect to Being. Aristotle explains this by adding in the cited statement to the question, What is being? the explanation: "This is what Beingness is"; in translation: "This (namely, *ti to on*) means, what is the Beingness of being?" The Being of being rests in the Beingness. But this—the *ousia* [Beingness]—Plato calls *idea* and Aristotle the *energeia* [actuality].

At the moment, it is not yet necessary to explain more exactly what Aristotle means by *energeia* and to what extent the *ousia* [Beingness] can be determined by the *energeia*. Now it is only important that we note how Aristotle circumscribes philosophy in its nature. In the first book of the *Metaphysics* (*Met.* A 2, 982 b 9 sq) he makes the following statement: Philosophy is speculative knowledge of the first principles and causes. *Epistêmê* is commonly translated as "science." This is misleading because we are only too apt to let the modern conception of "science" infiltrate. The

lassen. Die Übersetzung von ἐπιστήμη durch „Wissenschaft" ist auch dann irrig, wenn wir „Wissenschaft" in dem philosophischen Sinne verstehen, den Fichte, Schelling und Hegel meinen. Das Wort ἐπιστήμη leitet sich von dem Participium ἐπιστάμενος her. So heißt der Mensch, insofern er für etwas zuständig und geschickt ist (Zuständigkeit im Sinne von appartenance). Die Philosophie ist ἐπιστήμη τις, eine Art von Zuständigkeit, θεωρητική, die das θεωρεῖν vermag, d. h. auszuschauen nach etwas und dieses, wonach sie Ausschau hält, in den Blick zu nehmen und im Blick zu behalten. Die Philosophie ist darum ἐπιστήμη θεωρητική. Was aber ist das, was sie in den Blick nimmt?

Aristoteles sagt es, indem er die πρῶται ἀρχαί καί αἰτίαι nennt. Man übersetzt: „die ersten Gründe und Ursachen" – nämlich des Seienden. Die ersten Gründe und Ursachen machen so das Sein des Seienden aus. Es wäre nach zweieinhalb Jahrtausenden an der Zeit, darüber nachzudenken, was denn das Sein des Seienden mit so etwas wie „Grund" und „Ursache" zu schaffen hat.

translation of *epistêmê* by "science" is also wrong if we understand "science" in the philosophical sense of Fichte, Schelling, and Hegel. The word *epistêmê* is derived from the participle *epistamenos* [one who knows how]. That is what a man is called when he is competent and apt in something (competent in the sense of *appartenance* [aptitude]). Philosophy is *epistêmê tis*, a kind of competence, *theôrêtikê*, which is capable of *theôrein* [speculating], that is, of being on the lookout for something and of seizing and holding in its glance what it is on the lookout for. Philosophy, therefore, is *epistêmê theôrêtikê* [speculative knowledge]. But what is it that it seizes in its glance?

Aristotle says what it is when he names the *prôtai archai kai aitiai*. This may be translated as "the first principles and causes" namely, of being. The first principles and causes thus constitute the Being of being. After two-and-a-half thousand years it would seem to be about time to consider what the Being of being has to do with such things as "principles" and "causes."

In welchem Sinne wird das Sein gedacht, daß dergleichen wie „Grund" und „Ursache" sich dazu eignen, das seiend-Sein des Seienden zu prägen und zu übernehmen?

Doch wir achten jetzt auf anderes. Der angeführte Satz des Aristoteles sagt uns, wohin das, was man seit Platon „Philosophie" nennt, unterwegs ist. Der Satz gibt eine Auskunft darüber, was das ist – die Philosophie. Die Philosophie ist eine Art von Zuständigkeit, die dazu befähigt, das Seiende in den Blick zu nehmen, nämlich im Hinblick darauf, *was es ist,* insofern es Seiendes ist.

Die Frage, die unserem Gespräch die fruchtbare Unruhe und Bewegung geben und dem Gespräch die Wegrichtung weisen soll, die Frage: was ist Philosophie? hat Aristoteles schon beantwortet. Also ist unser Gespräch nicht mehr nötig. Es ist zu Ende, bevor es begonnen hat. Man wird sogleich erwidern, daß die Aussage des Aristoteles über das, was die Philosophie ist, keineswegs die einzige Antwort auf unsere Frage sein kann. Im günstigen Fall ist sie *eine* Antwort unter vielen anderen. Mit

58

In what sense is Being conceived that such things as "principle" and "cause" are qualified to set their seal upon beings and take possession of them?

But now we note something else. The phrase of Aristotle cited above tells us in what direction that which since Plato has been called "philosophy" is going. Philosophy is a kind of aptness which makes it possible to see being in respect to *what* it *is* in so far as it is being.

The question which is to give our discussion fruitful unrest and movement and to indicate the direction it is to take, the question, "What is philosophy?" Aristotle has already answered. Therefore, our discussion is no longer necessary. It is at an end before it has begun. The immediate reply to this will be that Aristotle's statement as to what philosophy is can by no means be the only answer to our question. To state it favorably, it is *one* answer among many others. With

Hilfe der aristotelischen Kennzeichnung der Philosophie kann man zwar sowohl das Denken vor Aristoteles und Platon als auch die Philosophie nach der Zeit des Aristoteles vorstellen und auslegen. Indes wird man mit Leichtigkeit darauf hinweisen, daß sich die Philosophie selbst und die Art, wie sie ihr eigenes Wesen vorstellt, in den folgenden zwei Jahrtausenden vielfältig gewandelt haben. Wer wollte dies leugnen? Wir dürfen aber auch nicht darüber hinweggehen, daß die Philosophie von Aristoteles bis Nietzsche gerade auf dem Grunde dieser Wandlungen und durch sie hindurch dieselbe bleibt. Denn die Verwandlungen sind die Bürgschaft für die Verwandtschaft im Selben.

Damit behaupten wir keineswegs, die aristotelische Definition der Philosophie gelte absolut. Sie ist nämlich schon innerhalb der Geschichte des griechischen Denkens nur eine bestimmte Auslegung des griechischen Denkens und dessen, was diesem aufgegeben wurde. Die aristotelische Kennzeichnung der Philosophie läßt sich in keinem Falle auf das Denken des Heraklit

the help of the Aristotelian characterization of philosophy one can, to be sure, conceive and interpret both the thinking before Aristotle and Plato, as well as philosophy after the time of Aristotle. However, it will be pointed out with ease that philosophy itself and the way in which it conceives its own nature have changed frequently in the subsequent two thousand years. Who would deny this? At the same time we ought not, however, overlook the fact that philosophy from Aristotle to Nietzsche, precisely because of these changes throughout their course, has remained the same. For the transformations are the warranty for the kinship in the same.

By saying this we by no means maintain that the Aristotelian definition of philosophy is absolutely valid. Even within the history of Greek thought it is only one particular interpretation of Greek thinking and of the task assigned to it. The Aristotelian characterization of philosophy cannot in any case be transferred back to the thinking of Heraclitus and Parmenides.

und des Parmenides zurückübertragen; dagegen ist die aristotelische Definition der Philosophie allerdings eine freie Folge des frühen Denkens und dessen Abschluß. Ich sage: eine freie Folge, weil auf keine Weise einsichtig gemacht werden kann, daß die einzelnen Philosophien und die Epochen der Philosophie im Sinne der Notwendigkeit eines dialektischen Prozesses auseinander hervorgehen.

Was ergibt sich aus dem Gesagten für unseren Versuch, in einem Gespräch die Frage: Was ist das – die Philosophie? zu behandeln? Zunächst das eine: wir dürfen uns nicht nur an die Definition des Aristoteles halten. Daraus entnehmen wir das andere: wir müssen die früheren und die späteren Definitionen der Philosophie uns vergegenwärtigen. Und dann? Dann werden wir durch eine vergleichende Abstraktion dasjenige herausstellen, was das Gemeinsame aller Definitionen ist. Und dann? Dann werden wir zu einer leeren Formel gelangen, die auf jede Art von Philosophie paßt. Und dann? Dann werden wir von einer Antwort auf unsere Frage so weit

On the contrary, the Aristotelian definition of philosophy is, to be sure, a free consequence of early thinking and its conclusion. I say "a free consequence" because in no way can it be seen that individual philosophies and epochs of philosophy have emerged from one another in the sense of the necessity of a dialectic process.

What is the result from what has been said for our attempt in a discussion to treat the question, "What is philosophy?" First of all this one thing: we must not adhere only to Aristotle's definition. From this we deduce the second point: we must realize the earlier and later definitions of philosophy. And then? Then, through a comparative abstraction, we shall reduce them to the common denominator of all the definitions. And then? Then we shall arrive at an empty formula which fits every kind of philosophy. And then? Then we shall be as far removed as possible from an answer

als nur möglich entfernt sein. Weshalb kommt es dahin? Weil wir durch das soeben erwähnte Verfahren nur historisch die vorliegenden Definitionen sammeln und sie in eine allgemeine Formel auflösen. Dies alles läßt sich in der Tat mit großer Gelehrsamkeit und mit Hilfe richtiger Feststellungen durchführen. Wir brauchen uns dabei nicht im geringsten auf die Philosophie in der Weise einzulassen, daß wir dem Wesen der Philosophie nach-denken. Wir gewinnen auf solche Weise vielfältige und gründliche und sogar nützliche Kenntnisse darüber, wie man die Philosophie im Verlaufe ihrer Geschichte vorgestellt hat. Aber wir gelangen auf diesem Wege niemals zu einer echten, d. h. legitimen Antwort auf die Frage: Was ist das – die Philosophie? Die Antwort kann nur eine philosophierende Antwort sein, eine Antwort, die als Ant-wort in sich philosophiert. Doch wie sollen wir diesen Satz verstehen? Inwiefern kann eine Antwort, und zwar insofern sie Ant-wort ist, philosophieren? Ich versuche dies jetzt vorläufig durch einige Hinweise aufzuhellen. Was gemeint ist, wird unser Gespräch immer

64

to our question. Why does it come to this? Because in proceeding thus we are only collecting by historical methodology the definitions at hand and resolving them into a general formula. All of this can, indeed, be carried out with great erudition and the help of correct verifications. In so doing we do not in the least have to enter into philosophy in such a manner as to contemplate the nature of philosophy. In such a manner we acquire manifold, thorough, and even useful knowledge about how philosophy has been presented in the course of history. But on this path we never reach a genuine, that is, a legitimate answer to the question, "What is philosophy?" The answer can only be a philosophizing answer which, as a response, philosophizes in itself. But how are we to understand this statement? In which way can an answer, and particularly in so far as it is a response, philosophize? I shall now try provisionally to clarify this by a few suggestions. What is meant will disturb our discus-

wieder beunruhigen. Es wird sogar der Prüfstein dafür sein, ob unser Gespräch ein wahrhaft philosophisches werden darf. Dies steht durchaus nicht in unserer Macht.

Wann ist die Antwort auf die Frage: was ist das – die Philosophie? eine philosophierende? Wann philosophieren wir? Offenbar erst dann, wenn wir mit den Philosophen ins Gespräch kommen. Dazu gehört, daß wir mit ihnen dasjenige durchsprechen, wovon sie sprechen. Dieses miteinander-Durchsprechen dessen, was immer wieder als das Selbe die Philosophen eigens angeht, ist das Sprechen, das λέγειν im Sinne des διαλέγεσθαι, das Sprechen als Dialog. Ob der Dialog notwendig eine Dialektik ist und wann, dies lassen wir offen.

Eines ist es, Meinungen der Philosophen festzustellen und zu beschreiben. Ein ganz anderes ist es, das, was sie sagen, und d. h. das, wovon sie sagen, mit ihnen durchzusprechen.

Gesetzt also, die Philosophen sind vom Sein des Seienden daraufhin angesprochen, daß sie sagen, was das Seiende sei, insofern es ist, dann muß auch unser Ge-

sion again and again. It will even be the touchstone to determine whether our discussion may become truly philosophical. This is by no means within our power.

When is the answer to the question, "What is philosophy?" a philosophizing one? When do we philosophize? Obviously only when we enter into a discussion with philosophers. This implies that we talk through with them that about which they speak. This mutual talking through of what always anew peculiarly concerns philosophers as being the Same, that is. talking, *legein,* in the sense of *dialegethai* [conversing], is talking as dialogue. If and when dialogue is necessarily dialectic, we leave open.

It is one thing to determine and describe the opinions of philosophers. It is an entirely different thing to talk through with them what they are saying, and that means, that of which they speak.

Thus, if we assume that the Being of being addresses itself to philosophers to the extent that they state what being is, in so far as it is, then our discus-

spräch mit den Philosophen vom Sein des Seienden angesprochen werden. Wir selber müssen dem, wohin die Philosophie unterwegs ist, durch unser Denken entgegenkommen. Unser Sprechen muß dem, wovon die Philosophen angesprochen sind, ent-sprechen. Wenn uns dieses Ent-sprechen glückt, dann ant-worten wir im echten Sinne auf die Frage: Was ist das – die Philosophie? Das deutsche Wort „antworten" bedeutet eigentlich soviel wie ent-sprechen. Die Antwort auf unsere Frage erschöpft sich nicht in einer Aussage, die auf die Frage mit einer Feststellung darüber erwidert, was man sich bei dem Begriff „Philosophie" vorzustellen habe. Die Antwort ist keine erwidernde Aussage (n'est pas une réponse), die Antwort ist vielmehr die Ent-sprechung (la correspondance), die dem Sein des Seienden entspricht. Doch sogleich möchten wir wissen, was denn das Charakteristische der Antwort im Sinne der Entsprechung ausmacht. Allein zuerst liegt alles daran, daß wir in eine Entsprechung gelangen, bevor wir die Theorie darüber aufstellen.

sion with philosophers must also be addressed by the Being of being. We must then ourselves, through our thinking, go to meet philosophy on the path it is traveling. Our speaking must co-respond to that which addresses the philosophers. If this co-responding is successful for us, then, in the true sense of the word, we respond to the question, "What is philosophy?" The German word *antworten* [answer to] actually means the same as *ent-sprechen* [to respond]. The answer to our question is not exhausted in an affirmation which answers to the question by determining what we are to understand by the concept "philosophy." The answer is not a reply (*n'est pas une réponse*), the answer is rather the co-respondence (*la correspondance*) which responds to the Being of being. Yet, we should like at the same time to know what constitutes the characteristic feature of the answer in the sense of co-respondence. But everything first depends upon our attaining a co-respondence before we set up a theory about it.

69

Die Antwort auf die Frage: Was ist das – die Philosophie? besteht darin, daß wir dem entsprechen, wohin die Philosophie unterwegs ist. Und das ist: das Sein des Seienden. In solchem Entsprechen hören wir von Anfang an auf das, was die Philosophie uns schon zugesprochen hat, die *Philosophie*, d. h. die griechisch verstandene φιλοσοφία. Deshalb gelangen wir nur *so* in die Entsprechung, d. h. zur Antwort auf unsere Frage, daß wir im Gespräch mit dem bleiben, wohin uns die Überlieferung der Philosophie ausliefert, d. h. befreit. Wir finden die Antwort auf die Frage, was die Philosophie sei, nicht durch historische Aussagen über die Definitionen der Philosophie, sondern durch das Gespräch mit dem, was sich uns als Sein des Seienden überliefert hat.

Dieser Weg zur Antwort auf unsere Frage ist kein Bruch mit der Geschichte, keine Verleugnung der Geschichte, sondern eine Aneignung und Verwandlung des Überlieferten. Solche Aneignung der Geschichte ist mit dem Titel „Destruktion" gemeint. Der Sinn dieses Wortes ist in „Sein und Zeit" klar umschrieben (§ 6). Destruktion

70

The answer to the question, "What is philosophy?" consists in our corresponding to [answering to] that towards which philosophy is on the way. And that is—the Being of being. In such a correspondence we listen from the very outset to that which philosophy has already said to us, *philosophy*, that is, *philosophia* understood in the Greek sense. That is why we attain correspondence, that is, an answer to our question, only *when* we remain in conversation with that to which the tradition of philosophy delivers us, that is, liberates us. We find the answer to the question, "What is philosophy?" not through historical assertions about the definitions of philosophy but through conversing with that which has been handed down to us as the Being of being.

This path to the answer to our question is not a break with history, no repudiation of history, but is an adoption and transformation of what has been handed down to us. Such an adoption of history is what is meant by the term "destruction." The meaning of this word has been clearly described in *Sein und Zeit* (§6). Destruction does not mean destroying

71

bedeutet nicht Zerstören, sondern Abbauen, Abtragen und Auf-die-Seite-stellen – nämlich die nur historischen Aussagen über die Geschichte der Philosophie. Destruktion heißt: unser Ohr öffnen, freimachen für das, was sich uns in der Überlieferung als Sein des Seienden zuspricht. Indem wir auf diesen Zuspruch hören, gelangen wir in die Entsprechung.

Aber während wir dies sagen, hat sich dagegen schon ein Bedenken gemeldet. Es lautet: Müssen wir uns denn erst darum bemühen, in eine Entsprechung zum Sein des Seienden zu gelangen? Sind wir, die Menschen, nicht immer schon in einer solchen Entsprechung, und zwar nicht nur de facto, sondern aus unserem Wesen? Macht diese Entsprechung nicht den Grundzug unseres Wesens aus?

So steht es in Wahrheit. Wenn es aber so steht, dann können wir nicht mehr sagen, daß wir erst in diese Entsprechung gelangen sollen. Und dennoch sagen wir dies mit Recht. Denn wir halten uns zwar immer und überall in der Entsprechung zum Sein des Seienden auf, gleichwohl achten wir nur selten auf den Zuspruch des

but dismantling, liquidating, putting to one side the merely historical assertions about the history of philosophy. Destruction means—to open our ears, to make ourselves free for what speaks to us in tradition as the Being of being. By listening to this interpellation we attain the correspondence.

But while we are saying this, a doubt has already made itself felt. It is this—must we first make an effort to reach a correspondence with the Being of being? Are we, humans, not always already in such a correspondence, and, what is more, not only *de facto*, but by virtue of our nature? Does not this correspondence constitute the fundamental trait of our nature?

This is, indeed, the case. But if this is the case, then we can no longer say that we first have to attain this correspondence. And yet we are right in saying so. For, to be sure, although we do remain always and everywhere in correspondence to the Being of being, we, nevertheless, rarely pay attention to the

Seins. Die Entsprechung zum Sein des Seienden bleibt zwar stets unser Aufenthalt. Doch nur zuzeiten wird sie zu einem von uns eigens übernommenen und sich entfaltenden Verhalten. Erst wenn dies geschieht, entsprechen wir erst eigentlich dem, was die Philosophie angeht, die zum Sein des Seienden unterwegs ist. Das Entsprechen zum Sein des Seienden ist die Philosophie; sie ist es aber erst dann und nur dann, wenn das Entsprechen sich eigens vollzieht, dadurch sich entfaltet und diese Entfaltung ausbaut. Dieses Entsprechen geschieht auf verschiedene Weise, je nachdem der Zuspruch des Seins spricht, je nachdem er gehört oder überhört wird, je nachdem das Gehörte gesagt oder geschwiegen wird. Unser Gespräch kann Gelegenheiten ergeben, darüber nachzudenken.

Jetzt versuche ich nur, ein Vorwort zum Gespräch zu sagen. Ich möchte das bisher Dargelegte zurückbiegen auf das, was wir im Anschluß an das Wort von André Gide über die „schönen Gefühle" gestreift haben. Φιλοσοφία ist das eigens vollzogene Entsprechen, das

appeal of Being. The correspondence to the Being of being does, to be sure, always remain our abode. But only at times does it become an unfolding attitude specifically adopted by us. Only when this happens do we really correspond to that which concerns phisophy which is on the way towards the Being of being. Philosophy is the correspondence to the Being of being, but not until, and only when, the correspondence is actually fulfilled and thereby unfolds itself and expands this unfoldment. This correspondence occurs in different ways according to how the appeal of Being speaks, according to whether it is heard or not heard, and according to whether what is heard is said or is kept silent. Our discussion can result in opportunities to reflect upon it.

Now I shall only try to express a foreword to the discussion. I should like to turn the discussion back to what we touched upon in connection with André Gide's words about "fine sentiments." *Philosophia* is the expressly accomplished correspondence which

spricht, insofern es auf den Zuspruch des Seins des Seienden achtet. Das Ent-sprechen hört auf die Stimme des Zuspruchs. Was sich als Stimme des Seins uns zuspricht, be-stimmt unser Entsprechen. „Entsprechen" heißt dann: be-stimmt sein, être disposé, nämlich vom Sein des Seienden her. Dis-posé bedeutet hier wörtlich: auseinander-gesetzt, gelichtet und dadurch in die Bezüge zu dem versetzt, was ist. Das Seiende als solches bestimmt das Sprechen in einer Weise, daß sich das Sagen abstimmt (accorder) auf das Sein des Seienden. Das Entsprechen ist notwendig und immer, nicht nur zufällig und bisweilen, ein gestimmtes. Es ist in einer Gestimmtheit. Und erst auf dem Grunde der Gestimmtheit (disposition) empfängt das Sagen des Entsprechens seine Präzision, seine Be-stimmtheit.

Als ge-stimmtes und be-stimmtes ist das Entsprechen wesenhaft in einer Stimmung. Dadurch ist unser Verhalten jeweils so oder so gefügt. Die so verstandene Stimmung ist keine Musik von zufällig auftauchenden Gefühlen, die das Entsprechen nur begleiten. Wenn wir

speaks in so far as it considers the appeal of the Being of being. The correspondence listens to the voice of the appeal. What appeals to us as the voice of Being evokes our correspondence. "Correspondence" then means: being de-termined, *être disposé* by that which comes from the Being of being. *Dis-posé* here means literally set-apart, cleared, and thereby placed in relationship with what is. Being as such determines speaking in such a way that language is attuned (*accorder*) to the Being of being. Correspondence is necessary and is always attuned, and not just accidentally and occasionally. It is in an attunement. And only on the basis of the attunement (*disposition*) does the language of correspondence obtain its precision, its tuning.

As something tuned and attuned, correspondence really exists in a tuning.[5] Through it our attitude is adjusted sometimes in this, sometimes in that way. The tuning understood in this sense is not music of accidentally emerging feelings which only accom-

5. The translation of the word *Stimmung* by tuning implies also the idea of disposition. Heidegger shows that it is necessary to be disposed, or tuned, to a thought to understand it.

die Philosophie als das gestimmte Entsprechen kennzeichnen, dann wollen wir keineswegs das Denken dem
zufälligen Wechsel und den Schwankungen von Gefühls-
zuständen ausliefern. Vielmehr handelt es sich einzig
darum, darauf hinzuweisen, daß jede Präzision des Sagens in einer Disposition des Entsprechens gründet, des
Entsprechens sage ich, der correspondance, im Achten
auf den Zuspruch.

Vor allem aber ist der Hinweis auf die wesenhafte Gestimmtheit des Entsprechens nicht erst eine moderne
Erfindung. Schon die griechischen Denker, Platon und
Aristoteles, haben darauf aufmerksam gemacht, daß die
Philosophie und das Philosophieren in die Dimension
des Menschen gehören, die wir die Stimmung (im Sinne
der Ge-stimmtheit und Be-stimmtheit) nennen.

Platon sagt (Theätet 155 d): μάλα γὰρ φιλοσόφου τοῦτο τὸ
πάθος, τὸ θαυμάζειν. οὐ γὰρ ἄλλη ἀρχὴ φιλοσοφίας ἢ αὕτη.

„Gar sehr nämlich ist eines Philosophen dieses das πάθος
– das Erstaunen; nicht nämlich ein anderes beherrschen-
des Woher der Philosophie gibt es als dieses."

78

pany the correspondence. If we characterize philosophy as tuned correspondence, then we by no means want to surrender thinking to the accidental changes and vaccilations of sentiments. It is rather solely a question of pointing out that every precision of language is grounded in a disposition of correspondence, of correspondence, I say, in heeding the appeal.

Above all, however, the reference to the essential disposition of correspondence is not a modern invention. The Greek thinkers, Plato and Aristotle, already drew attention to the fact that philosophy and philosophizing belong in the dimension of man which we call tuning (in the sense of tuning and attunement).

Plato says (*Theatet*, 155 d): "For this is especially the *pathos* [emotion] of a philosopher, to be astonished. For there is no other beginning of *philosophia* than this." "Very much is this especially the *pathos* of a philosopher, namely, to be astonished; for there is no other determining point of departure for philosophy than this."

Philosophical concepts must be grasped. This is possible only if the mind is attuned or disposed for the grasping of the idea. Therefore, the word tuning implies disposition. It is this disposition or tuning which makes possible the Being of being.

79

Das Erstaunen ist als πάθος die ἀρχή der Philosophie. Das griechische Wort ἀρχή müssen wir im vollen Sinne verstehen. Es nennt dasjenige, von woher etwas ausgeht. Aber dieses „von woher" wird im Ausgehen nicht zurückgelassen, vielmehr wird die ἀρχή zu dem, was das Verbum ἄρχειν sagt, zu solchem, was herrscht. Das πάθος des Erstaunens steht nicht einfach so am Beginn der Philosophie wie z. B. der Operation des Chirurgen das Waschen der Hände voraufgeht. Das Erstaunen trägt und durchherrscht die Philosophie.

Aristoteles sagt dasselbe (Met. A 2, 982 b 12 sq): διὰ γὰρ τὸ θαυμάζειν οἱ ἄνθρωποι καὶ νῦν καὶ τὸ πρῶτον ἤρξαντο φιλοσοφεῖν. „Durch das Erstaunen hindurch nämlich gelangten die Menschen jetzt sowohl als auch zuerst in den beherrschenden Ausgang des Philosophierens" (zu dem, von woher das Philosophieren ausgeht und was den Gang des Philosophierens durchgängig bestimmt).

Es wäre sehr oberflächlich und vor allem ungriechisch gedacht, wollten wir meinen, Platon und Aristoteles stellten hier nur fest, das Erstaunen sei die Ursache des.

80

Astonishment, as *pathos,* is the *archê* [the beginning] of philosophy. We must understand the Greek word *archê* [beginning] in its fullest sense. It names that from which something proceeds. But this "from where" is not left behind in the process of going out, but the beginning rather becomes that which the verb *archein* expresses, that which governs. The *pathos* of astonishment thus does not simply stand at the beginning of philosophy, as, for example, the washing of his hands precedes the surgeon's operation. Astonishment carries and pervades philosophy.

Aristotle says the same thing (*Met.* A 2, 982 b 12 sq): "For through astonishment men have begun to philosophize both in our times and at the beginning." "Through astonishment men have reached now, as well as at first, the determining path of philosophizing" (that from which philosophizing emanates and that which altogether determines the course of philosophizing).

It would be very superficial and, above all, very un-Greek, if we would believe that Plato and Aristotle are only determining here that astonishment is the

Philosophierens. Wären sie dieser Meinung, dann hieße das: irgendeinmal erstaunten die Menschen, nämlich über das Seiende, darüber, daß es ist und was es ist. Von diesem Erstaunen angetrieben, begannen sie zu philosophieren. Sobald die Philosophie in Gang gekommen war, wurde das Erstaunen als Anstoß überflüssig, so daß es verschwand. Es konnte verschwinden, da es nur ein Antrieb war. Aber: das Erstaunen ist ἀρχή – es durchherrscht jeden Schritt der Philosophie. Das Erstaunen ist πάθος. Wir übersetzen πάθος gewöhnlich durch passion, Leidenschaft, Gefühlswallung. Aber πάθος hängt zusammen mit πάσχειν, leiden, erdulden, ertragen, austragen, sich tragen lassen von, sich be-stimmen lassen durch. Es ist gewagt, wie immer in solchen Fällen, wenn wir πάθος durch Stimmung übersetzen, womit wir die Gestimmtheit und Be-stimmtheit meinen. Doch wir müssen diese Übersetzung wagen, weil sie allein uns davor bewahrt, πάθος in einem neuzeitlich-modernen Sinne psychologisch vorzustellen. Nur wenn wir πάθος als Stimmung (dis-position) verstehen, können wir auch

82

cause of philosophizing. If they were of this opinion, that would mean that at some time or other men were astonished especially about being and that it is and what it is. Impelled by this astonishment, they began to philosophize. As soon as philosophy was in progress, astonishment became superfluous as a propelling force so that it disappeared. It could disappear since it was only an impetus. However, astonishment is *archê*—it pervades every step of philosophy. Astonishment is *pathos*. We usually translate *pathos* with passion, ebullition of emotion. But *pathos* is connected with *paschein*, to suffer, endure, undergo, to be borne along by, to be determined by. It is risky, as it always is in such cases, if we translate *pathos* with tuning, by which we mean dis-position and determination. But we must risk this translation because it alone protects us from conceiving *pathos* in a very modern psychological sense. Only if we understand *pathos* as being attuned to, can we also characterize *thaumazein*,

das ϑαυμάζειν, das Erstaunen näher kennzeichnen. Im Erstaunen halten wir an uns (être en arrêt). Wir treten gleichsam zurück vor dem Seienden – davor, daß es ist und so und nicht anders ist. Auch erschöpft sich das Erstaunen nicht in diesem Zurücktreten vor dem Sein des Seienden, sondern es ist, als dieses Zurücktreten und Ansichhalten, zugleich hingerissen zu dem und gleichsam gefesselt durch das, wovor es zurücktritt. So ist das Erstaunen die Dis-position, in der und für die das Sein des Seienden sich öffnet. Das Erstaunen ist die Stimmung, innerhalb derer den griechischen Philosophen das Entsprechen zum Sein des Seienden gewährt wár.

Ganz anderer Art ist diejenige Stimmung, die das Denken bestimmte, die überlieferte Frage, was denn das Seiende sei, insofern es ist, auf eine neue Weise zu stellen und so eine neue Zeit der Philosophie zu beginnen. Descartes frägt in seinen Meditationen nicht nur und nicht zuerst τί τὸ ὄν – was ist das Seiende, insofern es ist? Descartes frägt: welches ist dasjenige Seiende, das im

84

astonishment, more exactly. In astonishment we re-strain ourselves (*être en arrêt*). We step back, as it were, from being, from the fact that it is as it is and not otherwise. And astonishment is not used up in this retreating from the Being of being, but, as this retreating and self-restraining, it is at the same time forcibly drawn to and, as it were, held fast by that from which it retreats. Thus, astonishment is dis-position in which and for which the Being of being unfolds. Astonishment is the tuning within which the Greek philosophers were granted the correspondence to the Being of being.

Of a very different sort is that tuning which made thinking decide to ask in a new way the traditional question of what being is, in so far as it is, and thus to begin a new era of philosophy. In his *Meditations* Descartes does not ask only, and does not ask first, *ti to on,* what being is, in so far as it is. Descartes asks what that being is that is true being in the sense

Sinne des ens certum das wahrhaft Seiende ist? Für Descartes hat sich inzwischen das Wesen der certitudo gewandelt. Denn im Mittelalter besagt certitudo nicht Gewißheit, sondern die feste Umgrenzung eines Seienden in dem, was es ist. Certitudo ist hier noch gleichbedeutend mit essentia. Dagegen bemißt sich für Descartes das, was wahrhaft *ist*, auf eine andere Weise. Ihm wird der Zweifel zu derjenigen Stimmung, in der die Gestimmtheit auf das ens certum, das in Gewißheit Seiende, schwingt. Die certitudo wird zu jener Festmachung des ens qua ens, die sich aus der Unbezweifelbarkeit des cogito (ergo) sum für das ego des Menschen ergibt. Dadurch wird das ego zum ausgezeichneten sub-iectum, und so tritt das Wesen des Menschen zum ersten Male in den Bereich der Subjektivität im Sinne der Egoität. Aus der Gestimmtheit auf diese certitudo empfängt das Sagen Descartes' die Bestimmtheit eines clare et distincte percipere. Die Stimmung des Zweifels ist die positive Zustimmung zur Gewißheit. Fortan wird die Gewißheit zur maßgebenden Form der Wahrheit. Die Stimmung

of the *ens certum*. For Descartes, the essence of *certitudo* has changed in the meanwhile, for in the Middle Ages *certitudo* does not signify certainty but the fixed delimitation of a being in that which it is. *Certitudo* here is still synonymous with *essentia*. On the other hand, for Descartes that which *is* true is measured in another way. For him doubt becomes that tuning in which the attunement [structure of determination] vibrates to the *ens certum*, i.e. being in certainty. *Certitudo* becomes a fixing of the *ens qua ens* which results from the unquestionability of the *cogito (ergo) sum* for man's ego. Thereby, the ego becomes the distinctive *sub-jectum* and thus the nature of man for the first time enters the realm of subjectivity in the sense of the ego. Out of the attunement to this *certitudo* the language of Descartes obtains the determination of a *clare et distincte percipere*. The tuning of doubt is the positive acquiescence in certainty. Henceforth, certainty becomes the determining form of truth. The tuning of confidence

der Zuversicht in die jederzeit erreichbare absolute Gewißheit der Erkenntnis bleibt das πάθος und somit die
ἀρχή der neuzeitlichen Philosophie.

Worin aber beruht das τέλος, die Vollendung der neuzeitlichen Philosophie, falls wir davon sprechen dürfen?
Ist dieses Ende durch eine andere Stimmung bestimmt?
Wo haben wir die Vollendung der neuzeitlichen Philosophie zu suchen? Bei Hegel oder erst in der Spätphilo-
sophie Schellings? Und wie steht es mit Marx und
Nietzsche? Treten sie schon aus der Bahn der neuzeitlichen Philosophie heraus? Wenn nicht, wie ist ihr
Standort zu bestimmen?

Es sieht so aus, als stellten wir nur historische Fragen.
Aber in Wahrheit bedenken wir das künftige Wesen
der Philosophie. Wir versuchen, auf die Stimme des
Seins zu hören. In welche Stimmung bringt sie das
heutige Denken? Die Frage ist kaum eindeutig zu beantworten. Vermutlich waltet eine Grundstimmung. Sie
bleibt uns aber noch verborgen. Dies wäre ein Zeichen
dafür, daß unser heutiges Denken noch nicht seinen

to the absolute certainty of knowledge which is attainable at all times is *pathos* and thus the *archê,* the beginning of modern philosophy.

However, on what does the *telos,* the completion of modern philosophy, depend, if we may speak of such. Is this end determined by another tuning? Where must we seek the completion of modern philosophy? In Hegel, or not until the later philosophy of Schelling? And how about Marx and Nietzsche? Do they already step out of the course of modern philosophy? If not, how can we determine their place?

It looks as though we were only posing historical questions. But, in truth, we are considering the future nature of philosophy. We are trying to listen to the voice of Being. Into what kind of tuning does this put contemporary thinking? The question can scarcely be answered unequivocally. Presumably a fundamental tuning prevails. It is, however, still hidden from us. This would indicate that our contemporary thinking has not yet found its unequivocal

eindeutigen Weg gefunden hat. Was wir antreffen, ist nur
dies: verschiedenartige Stimmungen des Denkens. Zweifel und Verzweiflung auf der einen, blinde Besessenheit
von ungeprüften Prinzipien auf der anderen Seite stehen gegeneinander. Furcht und Angst mischen sich mit
Hoffnung und Zuversicht. Oft und weithin sieht es so
aus, als sei das Denken nach der Art des räsonnierenden
Vorstellens und Rechnens von jeder Stimmung völlig
frei. Aber auch die Kälte der Berechnung, auch die prosaische Nüchternheit des Planens sind Kennzeichen
einer Gestimmtheit. Nicht nur dies; sogar die Vernunft,
die sich von allem Einfluß der Leidenschaften frei hält,
ist als Vernunft auf die Zuversicht in die logisch-mathematische Einsichtigkeit ihrer Prinzipien und Regeln gestimmt.

Das eigens übernommene und sich entfaltende Entsprechen, das dem Zuspruch des Seins des Seienden entspricht, ist die Philosophie. Was das ist – die Philosophie,
lernen wir nur kennen und wissen, wenn wir erfahren,
wie, auf welche Weise die Philosophie ist. Sie ist in der

path. What we come across is only this—various tunings of thinking. Doubt and despair, on the one hand, blind obsession by untested principles, on the other, conflict with one another. Fear and anxiety are mixed with hope and confidence. Often and widely, it looks as though thinking were a kind of reasoning conception and calculation completely free of any kind of tuning. But even the coldness of calculation, even the prosaic sobriety of planning are traits of an attunement. Not only that—even reason, which keeps itself free of every influence of the passions, is, as reason, attuned to confidence in the logically mathematical intelligence of its principles and rules.

The expressly adopted and unfolding correspondence which corresponds to the appeal of the Being of being is philosophy. We are introduced to and become acquainted with what philosophy is only when we learn how, in what manner, it is. It is in

Weise des Entsprechens, das sich abstimmt auf die Stimme des Seins des Seienden.

Dieses Ent-sprechen ist ein Sprechen. Es steht im Dienst der *Sprache*. Was dies heißt, ist für uns heute schwer zu verstehen; denn unsere geläufige Vorstellung von der Sprache hat seltsame Wandlungen durchgemacht. Ihnen zufolge erscheint die Sprache als ein Instrument des Ausdrucks. Demgemäß hält man es für richtiger zu sagen: die Sprache steht im Dienst des Denkens, statt: das Denken als Ent-sprechen steht im Dienst der Sprache. Vor allem aber ist die heutige Vorstellung von der Sprache so weit als nur möglich entfernt von der griechischen Erfahrung der Sprache. Den Griechen offenbart sich das Wesen der Sprache als der λόγος. Doch was heißt λόγος und λέγειν? Wir beginnen erst heute langsam, durch die mannigfaltigen Auslegungen des λόγος auf sein anfängliches griechisches Wesen hindurchzublikken. Indes können wir weder zu diesem Wesen der Sprache jemals wieder zurückkehren, noch können wir es einfach übernehmen. Wohl dagegen müssen wir mit

the manner of correspondence which is attuned to the voice of the Being of being.

This corresponding is a speaking. It is in the service of *language*. What this means is difficult for us to understand today, for our current conception of language has undergone strange changes. As a consequence, language appears as an instrument of expression. Accordingly, it is considered more correct to say that language is in the service of thinking rather than that thinking, as co-respondence, is in the service of language. Above all, the current conception of language is as far removed as possible from the Greek experience of language. To the Greeks the nature of language is revealed as the *logos*. But what do *logos* and *legein* mean? Only today are we slowly beginning to get a glimpse of its original Greek nature through the manifold interpretations of *logos*. However, we can neither ever again return to this nature of language, nor simply adopt it. On the con-

der griechischen Erfahrung der Sprache als λόγος in ein Gespräch kommen. Warum? Weil wir ohne eine zureichende Besinnung auf die Sprache niemals wahrhaft wissen, was die Philosophie als das gekennzeichnete Ent-sprechen, was die Philosophie als eine ausgezeichnete Weise des Sagens ist.

Weil nun aber die Dichtung, wenn wir sie mit dem Denken vergleichen, auf eine ganz andere und ausgezeichnete Weise im Dienst der Sprache steht, wird unser Gespräch, das der Philosophie nachdenkt, notwendig dahin geführt, das Verhältnis von Denken und Dichten zu erörtern. Zwischen beiden, Denken und Dichten, waltet eine verborgene Verwandtschaft, weil beide sich im Dienst der Sprache für die Sprache verwenden und verschwenden. Zwischen beiden aber besteht zugleich eine Kluft, denn sie „wohnen auf getrenntesten Bergen".

Nun könnte man mit gutem Recht verlangen, daß sich unser Gespräch auf die Frage nach der Philosophie beschränke. Diese Beschränkung wäre nur dann möglich

trary, we must probably enter into a conversation with the Greek experience of language as *logos*. Why? Because without a sufficient consideration of language, we never truly know what philosophy is as the distinguished co-respondence, nor what philosophy is as a distinctive manner of language.

But because poetry, if we compare it with thinking, is in the service of language in an entirely different and distinctive way, our discussion, which follows philosophy's thinking, necessarily leads to a discussion of the relationship between thinking and poetic creation. Between these two there exists a secret kinship because in the service of language both intercede on behalf of language and give lavishly of themselves. Between both there is, however, at the same time an abyss for they "dwell on the most widely separated mountains."

Now the request might quite justifiably be made that our discussion be restricted to the question about philosophy. This restriction would be possible and

und sogar notwendig, wenn sich im Gespräch ergeben sollte, daß die Philosophie nicht das ist, als was sie jetzt gedeutet wird: ein Entsprechen, das den Zuspruch des Seins des Seienden zur Sprache bringt.

Mit anderen Worten: unser Gespräch stellt sich nicht die Aufgabe, ein festes Programm abzuwickeln. Aber es möchte sich bemühen, alle, die daran teilnehmen, für eine Sammlung bereit zu machen, in der wir von dem angesprochen werden, was wir das Sein des Seienden nennen. Indem wir dies nennen, denken wir daran, was schon Aristoteles sagt:

„Das seiend-Sein kommt vielfältig zum Scheinen."*

Τὸ ὂν λέγεται πολλαχῶς.

---

* vgl. Sein und Zeit. § 7 B.

even necessary only if in the discussion it should turn out that philosophy is not that which it is now interpreted to be—a co-respondence which discusses the appeal of the Being of being.

In other words—our discussion does not set itself the task of winding up a fixed program. But it would like to prepare all who are participating for a gathering in which what we call the Being of being appeals to us. By naming this we are considering what Aristotle already says:

"Being-ness appears in many guises."[6] "Existence is revealed in many ways."

6. Cf *Sein und Zeit*, § 7B.